Physical Education

Key Stages 1, 2 and 3
First Year, 1992–93

The implementation of
the curricular requirements
of the Education Reform Act

A report from the Office
of Her Majesty's
Chief Inspector of Schools
London: HMSO

Office for Standards in Education
Elizabeth House
York Road
London SE1 7PH
Tel. 071-925 6800

© *Crown copyright 1993*
Applications for reproduction should be made to HMSO

ISBN 0 11 350029 7

CONTENTS

	Page
Introduction	1
Main Findings	2

THE REPORT

Teaching and Learning
Key Stages 1 and 2	5
Key Stage 3	6

Curriculum and Organisation
Key Stages 1 and 2	9
Key Stage 3	10

Assessment, Recording and Reporting
Key Stages 1 and 2	13
Key Stage 3	13

Staffing
Key Stages 1 and 2	15
Key Stage 3	15

Staff Development
Key Stages 1 and 2	17
Key Stage 3	17

Resources and Accommodation
Key Stages 1 and 2	19
Key Stage 3	19

Issues
21

	Page
Appendix	22

INTRODUCTION

This is the first report on physical education (PE) since its implementation as a National Curriculum foundation subject. The Attainment Target and Programmes of Study became statutory requirements for Year 1, Year 3 and Year 7 in maintained schools from 1 August 1992.

This report is concerned with the response of schools to the National Curriculum requirement for physical education during the school year 1992-1993. It is based on inspection by Her Majesty's Inspectors (HMI) of 105 primary schools, 100 secondary schools and 15 outdoor education centres. Overall 662 lessons in primary schools (Years 1 and 3), 337 lessons in secondary schools (Year 7), and 9 sessions in outdoor centres with Year 7 pupils were inspected.

The schools were not chosen to provide a statistically representative sample. Nevertheless, schools of all types, locations and sizes were inspected.

MAIN FINDINGS

Key Stages 1 and 2

- In about two-thirds of the lessons the standards the pupils achieved were satisfactory or better. There were no significant differences in standards between the two key stages (paragraph 1);

- Many class teachers lacked knowledge and expertise in teaching physical education; they needed more effective guidance to help improve the quality of their teaching (paragraphs 5, 29, 30, 35);

- Curricular planning has improved but assessment procedures were weakly developed (paragraphs 13, 24);

Key Stage 3

- Standards of achievement were satisfactory or better in 70 per cent of the lessons (paragraph 6);

- Over half of the lessons seen were in games. This area of activity continues to dominate the physical education programme although some adjustments have been made to achieve a better balance. Dance was not universally offered; when it was taught standards were usually high (paragraph 6);

- There was little evidence of schools' planning outdoor and adventurous activities although a few schools made good use of outdoor centres (6);

- The assessment, recording and reporting of pupils' progress in physical education were in the early days of development (paragraph 25);

- Overall there was a satisfactory understanding of both the general and the specific requirements of the National Curriculum. The teachers recognised the need to extend their range of teaching styles, and to give their pupils opportunities to plan and evaluate. Many were working hard to achieve this (paragraphs 12 and 16).

THE REPORT

TEACHING AND LEARNING

Key Stages 1 and 2

1. In Years 1 and 3 standards of achievement were satisfactory or better in about two-thirds of the lessons; just under one-third were good or very good. There were no significant differences in the standards achieved in the two Key Stages or in the different areas of activity.

2. In the best lessons the pupils showed a good understanding of the ways in which their bodies could move; they planned and evaluated their work effectively by exploring a range of options in response to a task and by selecting the most interesting or effective response. Some improved their performance after discussion with their teacher. Where standards achieved were less than satisfactory the pupils' movement responses showed little clarity in shape or contrast in dynamics (for example, varying speed, force and rhythm in movement), and had a limited range of movement ideas. Pupils were not involved in the planning and evaluating strands of the Attainment Target.

3. In the best lessons pupils worked independently and for sustained periods. Good relationships showed when pupils worked co-operatively in pairs or small groups, sharing equipment and apparatus. Pupils were generally well motivated and responded enthusiastically.

4. The most successful teaching was characterised by well-planned lessons with clear learning objectives. The teachers used constructive comment well, and demonstration was used effectively to improve the standard of the work. A good pace was set and time was used effectively. Good, safe practice was evident in the teachers' established routines.

5. The main weaknesses that characterised the one-third of lessons that were less than satisfactory were a lack of knowledge and expertise which led to a lack of confidence on the part of the teacher. Many of the poor lessons suffered from weak planning, inadequate organisation of pupils and equipment, and inefficient use of the pupils' time. Some of the teachers did not balance the use of aural and visual prompts to help the pupils to improve their skills, knowledge and understanding.

Key Stage 3

6. Standards were satisfactory or better in just over 70 per cent of the lessons in Year 7, including 10 per cent in which the standards achieved by pupils were very good. There was variation in the proportion of lessons seen in each of the areas of activity and in the standards achieved. Over half the lessons seen were in games and in the summer term for example, two-thirds of the lessons were in games; fewer than one in ten of these was very good although in three-quarters standards were satisfactory or better. Less than one-tenth of the lessons seen were in dance and of these one in six was very good and almost all were satisfactory or better. Of the few lessons seen in outdoor and adventurous activities in schools, standards were low often revealing a lack of planning and limited confidence on the part of teachers. The work seen at the outdoor education centres was generally of better quality and the pupils achieved standards varying from satisfactory to good. Standards in nearly two-thirds of athletics lessons were satisfactory or better, but in no lesson were they very good.

7. In the 10 per cent of lessons where high standards were achieved, the pupils showed good levels of individual skill and adapted their responses effectively, for example, in using different apparatus or responding to the changing circumstances of a game. Some of the pupils demonstrated effective planning in their positioning, anticipation, and structuring of sequences of movement. The progress of pupils was helped when they were encouraged to observe and analyse their own and other pupils'

movement. Many were good at applying agreed criteria for success, for example, in teaching a partner. This increased the challenge of the work.

8. In these successful lessons the pupils concentrated well on the task, listened carefully to the teacher's comments and practised diligently to improve their performance. They co-operated well in tasks involving partners, often adapting and modifying their responses and showing tolerance of each other's limitations. The pupils often worked independently and showed an emerging ability to observe work accurately and to give good oral comments on what they had seen. Poor quality learning was characterised by restlessness, poor concentration, passivity and lack of precision in approaches to answering tasks. Too often pupils showed limited ability to profit from previous learning in transferring skills to a new context.

9. Where the teaching was good, high expectations of pupils were held by the teachers, clear learning objectives were set, a good pace for learning was maintained and a range of demands were made on pupils using different teaching styles. In many of these lessons different tasks were set for pupils of different abilities. For example, in learning to play a game one teacher recognised that opposing teams of equal numbers was too high a level of competition for the development of some pupils' skill and tactical understanding. By organising unequal numbers of players in a small game, in this case four versus two, the teacher was able to provide these pupils with a more appropriate level of competition in which to develop their skill and understanding. Generally, adequate time was allowed for pupils to practise and the teachers intervened at appropriate moments and guided the pupils to improve the quality of their movement and the standards achieved. Opportunities were created for pupils to contribute to the planning and evaluation of their work.

10. Where standards were low the responses of the pupils were poorly co-ordinated. They produced consistent skilful movement only in prescribed and predictable circumstances. They could

reproduce routine sequences but their own attempts lacked originality or understanding of the task. Limited opportunities for planning and evaluating led to the development of limited skills in these aspects of the Attainment Target.

11. In the 30 per cent of lessons where the teaching was poor, learning objectives were not specified, teachers were reluctant to intervene, a relaxed pace was tolerated and expectations were modest. Some of the teachers had an inadequate grasp of the material and relied too heavily on a favoured style of teaching. Different work was rarely planned for pupils of different abilities and class organisation and control were weak. The Attainment Target in physical education includes pupils' ability to plan, to perform and to evaluate performance. Evidence of planning and evaluating was limited because too few opportunities were afforded to the pupils to demonstrate achievement in these aspects of the work. Most of the work was concerned with the performance of physical skills in a variety of contexts.

CURRICULUM AND ORGANISATION

Key Stages 1 and 2

12. At Key Stages 1 and 2 the teachers were following the non-statutory guidance and focused on gymnastics, dance and games, supplementing the weekly lessons in all three with blocks of swimming and/or simple athletics. The time allocation for physical education was adequate in most schools, although inconsistencies were observed between the timetabled provision for different classes within the same school.

13. Documentation was of variable quality, ranging from poor to good but overall curricular planning has improved. Many of the teachers relied on local education authority (LEA) guidelines and they were becoming familiar with the National Curriculum Programmes of Study. Too many teachers continued to plan work without taking sufficient account of their pupils' previous learning. The quality of much teaching could be improved through the greater sharing of staff expertise and better schemes of work to guide planning for progression. Physical education rarely featured in the school development plan. The termly plans made by class teachers often referred briefly to physical education but learning objectives were infrequently specified.

14. The schools were generally aware of the need to provide equal opportunities for both boys and girls. In a significant number of schools however, the boys and the girls were not given the opportunity to work together during games activities in Key Stage 2.

15. Extra-curricular activities took place in many of the schools and increasingly offered an opportunity for parents and other adults to become involved. Some of the schools had good links with clubs which provided opportunities for talented pupils, or those with keen interests, to pursue their preferred activities in their own time.

Key Stage 3

16. There was a strong link between the quality of the scheme of work and the quality of teaching and standards of work in the school. Good progress has been made in many secondary departments in adjusting their existing schemes of work to reflect the requirements of the National Curriculum. Most schemes of work included aims and objectives, teaching methods, resources and departmental routines as well as content. Even so, over half the schools visited in the autumn term had schemes of work which took no account of the National Curriculum.

17. Increasingly the schemes of work recommended teaching approaches and took account of the need to develop pupils' planning and evaluating skills as well as the more familiar performance skills. Sometimes team teaching was suggested so that staff might learn from each other's strengths. Only a few schemes however, made reference to the assessment of pupils' performance as an integral part of teaching.

18. Though generally adequate, the time allocated to physical education varied between seven and 12 per cent of the available curriculum time, which itself varied considerably. A further factor which had a bearing on calculating the time allocation was how the school treated dance and whether it fell within the allocation of time for the arts or within that for physical education.

19. The organisation of the curriculum varied in its effectiveness. The continuity and progression of pupils' learning was usually adversely affected by the allocation of short blocks of time to different activities. Some groupings of pupils were determined by their ability in other subjects and in some of the schools top sets and bottom sets were arbitrarily joined together to make a 'mixed ability' group for physical education. Such arrangements led to predictable difficulties in planning and in matching the teaching to meet what was often a very wide range of physical and intellectual ability in the class.

20. Where there were separate departments for boys' and girls' physical education, there was often different provision either in the balance of the areas of activity specified in the National Curriculum or in the teaching approaches used. It was not unusual for boys to have restricted access to some of the areas of activity compared with girls in the same school. The increasing frequency of mixed gender groupings has enabled girls to have a broader experience of games: many have been introduced to soccer and to basketball for the first time. Boys, however, frequently had less opportunity than girls to follow a progressive course in gymnastics and their access to dance was more limited.

21. There was evidence of increasing provision for pupils with special educational needs within physical education. Pupils were rarely disapplied from National Curriculum physical education. Some of the provision was quite separate from the mainstream experience, however, and did not provide the pupils with a balanced experience of physical activity and of ways of learning. Where efforts were made to adapt movement and the activities experienced by all pupils in order to allow participation within the class group, all pupils benefited from increased awareness. Some departments made good provision for pupils with physical disabilities through careful planning and by purchasing resources which were suitable for pupils with poor co-ordination, strength or flexibility.

22. Work in physical education was extended and enriched in most schools by a comprehensive programme of extra-curricular activities. These included representative team practices but also catered for non-selective teams and for interest groups in activities such as the Duke of Edinburgh's Award Scheme.

23. A good deal of time was given voluntarily by teachers in support of extra curricular work. Some of the schools had successfully developed partnerships with sports centres, sports development officers, dance officers and coaches. Where these partnerships worked well the teacher remained in overall control of pupils' learning. The preparation of appropriate

documentation for partnership arrangements helped the teachers to define clearly the separate roles of the teachers, the coaches and the trainers.

ASSESSMENT, RECORDING AND REPORTING

Key Stages 1 and 2

24. In Key Stages 1 and 2 there was some evidence of sound assessment, recording and reporting procedures in a few schools, but in the majority one or more of these procedures were inadequate. Many teachers lacked the confidence and expertise to establish clear criteria for the assessment of pupils' movement. The best teachers were skilful observers who had established clear criteria for assessing pupils' movement and used continuous assessment to give clear feedback to pupils. All the schools provided an end of year report; most contained comments on physical education but these were variable in quality and not always related to the National Curriculum in Years 1 and 3.

Key Stage 3

25. At Key Stage 3 many of the schools were still waiting for guidance which they believed would be available nationally. They were reluctant to change their present arrangements until the requirements were clarified. In the autumn term very few of the schools had arrangements in place for the assessment and recording of achievement although the school system for reporting to parents was usually well established. By the summer good progress had been made in some schools; many LEAs had produced helpful guidance for schools and staff were developing procedures which were based on a sound understanding of assessment as an integral part of teaching. Some LEA guidance on curriculum planning lacked parallel advice on assessing learning and reinforced the view of many teachers that assessment is a separate and subsequent activity.

26. In general, too many of the schools were attempting to do too much. In one school the teachers assessed pupils every six weeks. This reduced the effectiveness of teaching time and

resulted in an over-complex recording system. Many schools focused on pupils' attitudes and effort and did not assess standards of attainment at all.

27. The teachers were more confident in their judgements about performance than about pupils' ability to plan and evaluate performances. Where assessment criteria were established, they were often copied or adapted from in-service courses and not tailored to the planning of the programme.

28. Only a few of the schools were beginning to report on planning, performing and evaluating rather than just on performance in the separate physical activities. Some departments made good use of self-assessment by pupils. There was some evidence that non-specialists had difficulty in implementing assessment procedures which had been developed by specialist teachers and which were dependent on subject knowledge and good skills of observation.

STAFFING

Key Stages 1 and 2

29. Physical education was taught primarily by the class teachers in Key Stage 1 and 2. Their expertise in physical education was variable. Where there was a designated curriculum leader more progress had been made in meeting National Curriculum requirements. In some schools the curriculum leader had been released from teaching their own class, often by the head teacher, to attend in-service education and training (INSET) courses or to support colleagues in their teaching of the subject.

30. Some class teachers had only a rudimentary initial training in the subject. They lacked confidence in allowing pupils the freedom to explore and plan their own movement particularly in what were considered to be potentially hazardous situations involving large apparatus. They had little understanding of how to build progressively on pupils' responses. Many were more secure working within the structure of a simple game or with routine floor exercises.

31. Those curriculum co-ordinators who had studied physical education as their main subject during initial training were more confident in their approach to planning, teaching and assessment. Too frequently, however, the schools had no explicit policy for using the skills of the subject co-ordinator.

Key Stage 3

32. Almost all the staff teaching physical education full-time in the secondary schools were qualified to teach the subject. Some teachers of other subjects who assisted on a part-time basis were qualified only to teach games. Some senior staff, whose initial qualification was in the subject and who contributed occasionally to the teaching, were not always familiar with the Programmes of Study.

33. In many schools where there have traditionally been two separate departments, with separate curricula for boys and girls, the National Curriculum has provided the catalyst for amalgamation of the departments and rationalisation of the curriculum. The teaching and learning was often strengthened by exploiting specialist expertise for the benefit of both boys and girls.

34. There was no evidence of recruitment difficulties in the subject but some LEAs made flexible use of fixed-term contracts in the appointment of advisory teachers, sports and dance development officers and outdoor education co-ordinators to support the work of teachers.

STAFF DEVELOPMENT

Key Stages 1 and 2

35. Some of the teachers did not recognise that skills which they demonstrated with confidence in the classroom were equally appropriate in physical education. Some successful INSET was undertaken in schools where the staff worked together on the development of detailed guidelines for the subject assisted by a knowledgable curriculum leader. This resulted in well-managed and carefully co-ordinated programmes throughout the school. In other schools rapid progress had been made when the class teacher worked alongside an advisory teacher setting tasks and observing pupils moving.

36. The greatest problem that many schools had was in knowing what INSET was appropriate to their needs. The advice and support traditionally available from the LEA were diminishing and the schools had difficulty in evaluating the expertise and advice available to help them to plan and implement the Programmes of Study in their own circumstances.

Key Stage 3

37. Some excellent staff development has been achieved by individual departments in reviewing their schemes of work in the light of the National Curriculum. Such reviews were frequently all-embracing, involving a reconsideration of the rationale for the subject, the approaches to teaching and learning, the balance of the curriculum and the provision for the full ability range. The quality of professional debate in such departments was of a high order. Too many departments, however, found it very difficult to begin on their own development without some impetus from outside. They have struggled to identify their own needs and have found it even more difficult to meet them.

38. The most commonly expressed need was for support in developing procedures for assessment, recording and reporting. This need was not being met. In some LEAs clusters of schools have begun to meet regularly to support each other in curriculum development.

RESOURCES AND ACCOMMODATION

Key Stages 1 and 2

39. There was usually sufficient basic equipment for pupils in Key Stages 1 and 2. In some of the schools more appropriate apparatus was needed for the Key Stage 1 pupils. When resources were less than satisfactory it was sometimes due to shortage of finance, and on other occasions due to a lack of vision of what was required. Some primary schools still had very heavy gymnastic equipment which Key Stage 1 pupils, in particular, could not manage by themselves.

40. In the majority of the primary schools accommodation was adequate to meet the requirements of the National Curriculum Programme of Study. Indoor and outdoor facilities were available; many of the schools had both grass and hard play areas. A large proportion of the schools visited had access to local swimming pools or learner pools on-site. Some of the schools formed consortia and planned joint use of the pool at one school, sharing the maintenance costs. Special schools frequently featured in such arrangements. In many LEAs provision for swimming had been made ahead of the statutory requirement. Provision for outdoor and adventurous activities was generally less well advanced, although some of the schools had made good use of LEA residential centres.

Key Stage 3

41. In the secondary schools the provision of resources and equipment was satisfactory. Resources available to physical education departments were often supplemented by other funds such as those generated by parent-teacher associations. There was a wide variation in capitation and also a wide variation in what the allocation had to cover. In some of the schools transport to matches taking place outside school time was supported by departmental funds; in others there was unlimited access to

the school minibus. In some schools the purchase of specific equipment has improved the teaching of some activities, such as gymnastics, or has improved the experience for pupils with special needs, for example by providing a hoist for the swimming pool. There was evidence of increasing use of computers, video cameras and video playback facilities, the latter occasionally being used for assessment purposes.

42. Most of the secondary schools had sufficient accommodation to teach the National Curriculum, though some of this was in a poor condition. Outdoor playing areas were often extensive though the quality of drainage could sometimes restrict use. Provision for indoor work varied considerably; indoor spaces were increasingly lost for examinations and tests and this frequently restricted the balance of the physical education programme. Storage space was often a problem (except where new sports halls had been built). Changing facilities were barely adequate for the size of groups which used them and were often inadequately cleaned. Sites at some distance from the main school buildings were often under-used.

43. Recurrent safety issues included poor storage of equipment; litter (particularly glass and cans chopped-up by gang-mowers) and dog faeces on playing areas; loose surfaces on tennis courts and broken perimeter netting; low ceilings for trampolining and slippery floors in gymnasia and showers. Changes in contracts have a mixed impact.

ISSUES

44. The introduction of the National Curriculum has led both primary and secondary schools to review their teaching practices and the range and balance of their programmes. There is considerable goodwill among teachers to improve the quality of teaching and provision for pupils' physical education. A number of issues remain. Some are shared by all Key Stages and others are specific to the primary or the secondary phase:

- support is needed for primary teachers in developing long-term teaching plans which include the means of assessing pupils' progress;

- there is a need for better guidance on assessment, recording and reporting for teachers of all Key Stages;

- there is a need for INSET materials of good quality for use in school-based staff development;

- a better balance of time is required to cover adequately the different areas of activity taught in the Programmes of Study;

- programmes taught at Key Stage 3 are frequently too fragmented and need better continuity in teaching and learning;

- teachers need to give more emphasis to the planning and evaluating components of the Attainment Target. This will require them to diversify the range of teaching styles they use;

- teachers need further guidance on the development of programmes in outdoor and adventurous activity.

APPENDIX

There is one Attainment Target – Physical Education – which encompasses the strands of performing, and planning and evaluating performance.

There are both general and activity specific Programmes of Study. The general Programmes of Study provide End of Key Stage statements and examples to guide teachers' planning. The activity specific Programmes of Study are defined as six aspects of activity through which pupils develop the competence to perform in a range of movement contexts, and learn to plan and evaluate their own performances and those of others. These six aspects are:

- athletic activities;
- dance;
- games;
- gymnastic activities;
- outdoor and adventurous activities;
- swimming.

Requirements relating to the areas of activity vary according to Key Stages:

Swimming must be included at Key Stage 1 or Key Stage 2 but there is no requirement that it be included in both. Thereafter, all pupils in Key Stages 1 and 2 should cover all of the remaining five areas of activity.

In Key Stage 3 pupils should pursue a minimum of four areas of activity, with games compulsory each year and at least three other areas of activity from dance, athletics, gymnastics, and outdoor and adventurous activity.

In Key Stage 4 those not studying the General Certificate of Secondary Education in physical education or dance or any other related area should study at least two activities. These may be drawn from the same area or two different areas.